CLOSE to HEAVEN

Fifty years
of Purgatory

OPSW

Copyright © 2015 Center of Southwest Studies
Fort Lewis College
1000 Rim Drive
Durango, Colorado 81301
970-247-7456
Swcenter.fortlewis.edu

Published and distributed in collaboration with Purgatory Resort

Close to Heaven: Fifty Years of Purgatory
Center of Southwest Studies, Occasional Papers of the Southwest no. 6
ISBN: 978-0-9963932-0-1
Library of Congress Control Number: 2015954445

Contributing Writers:
Gary Derck
Jay T. Harrison
Robert McDaniel
Kim Oyler
Frederic B. Wildfang

Content and Copy Editor:
Elizabeth A. Green

Design and Layout:
Lisa Snider

Photo Coordination:
George Usinowicz

Printing:
CPC Solutions

On the cover:
On a typically sunny day Purgatory employee Linda (Outland) Mannix catches some rays in this photo for a late 1970s brochure.

Unless otherwise noted, the photos in this book are part of the "Purgatory Collection," known internally as collection P066, at the Center of Southwest Studies Delaney Southwest Research Library and Archives, Fort Lewis College.

This book is dedicated to
Raymond Twomey Duncan
1930-2015

*His vision, leadership, perseverance, and boundless belief in this place
have left an enduring legacy.*

*As Ray would readily agree, this book is also dedicated to the
amazing employees of Purgatory, past, present, and future
and to our wonderfully supportive community.*

Contents

Foreword

Dear Reader:

Purgatory is a wonderful and amazing resort. It was originally envisioned by my uncle Ray as a ski mountain for the local families of Durango, and it did not take long for families from the Southwest and the nation to discover its unique qualities as a fun and exciting winter and summer resort. It couldn't miss with the rare combination of great snow, quality trails and spectacular views. The resort quickly grew into a major part of the Durango economy, especially in winter, when local businesses needed tourists to survive.

The driving factor that made Purgatory special was the people who had the passion for the mountain and the commitment to make the resort a reality. From mountain planning, to building lifts, to cutting trails, to running the base support facilities—all who were involved in the early years of Purgatory put their hearts and souls into creating a distinctly family-friendly experience.

This spirit has persevered through the many improvements, changes, and challenges the resort has seen over the last fifty years and it is what keeps generations of families returning year after year. Other resorts might be bigger, more technical, or more convenient to get to, but there is something very special about Purgatory—an experience for families that is almost heavenly.

Thanks to all the employees, partners, guests, and loyal families who have helped create and sustain Purgatory over the past fifty years—and please continue to preserve the resort's special family atmosphere for many, many years to come.

Sincerely,

– Vincent J. Duncan Jr.
On behalf of
the Duncan Family

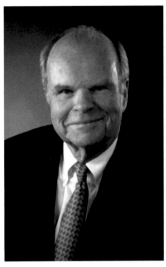

Raymond T. Duncan

Ray and Sally Duncan

Acknowledgments

Fifty years is a milestone worthy of celebration, especially when it involves a business that has grown without forgetting its roots in the community, all the while providing enjoyment for millions of people. The Center of Southwest Studies at Fort Lewis College is honored to play a part in that celebration with the publication of *Close to Heaven: Fifty Years of Purgatory.*

It would take several volumes to write about all the people and events that have shaped Purgatory through the past half century—more than space and time permit. This story represents not only those whose names you'll read, but countless more. We thank the people who made time to talk with us, and all the others whose contributions are represented here in spirit, if not by name.

Telling Purgatory's story in words and photos has been a collaborative effort involving a great many people.

A few years ago, Matt Langdon donated oral history tapes to the center. Matt's father Charlie Langdon chronicled Purgatory's early years in *Durango Ski* (published in1989 by Purgatory and reissued by Durango Herald Small Press in 2007). His recorded interviews encompass personal stories of people who were a part of the ski area from its inception.

More recently, George Usinowicz, a longtime Purgatory employee and skier, suggested that the Center develop a collection of Purgatory documents, images, and paraphernalia. He sought materials from locals and other Purgatory stalwarts near and far, gathering a unique collection, P066, for the Center's Delaney Southwest Research Library and Archives.

It was logical, then, that the Center of Southwest Studies would produce this book. Center Director Jay T. Harrison and supporter Frederic B. Wildfang conducted extensive research and wrote the preliminary text. They were joined by contributing writers Gary Derck (Purgatory's CEO since 2000), Kim Oyler (Purgatory's director of communications), and Robert McDaniel (retired Animas Museum director, historian, and longtime ski patrolman at Purgatory). Robert also fact-checked the entire text and tracked down numerous elusive details.

Gary also provided background information, source material, access to employees and ski area records, and financing for publication. Kim, Mike McCormack, and Jim "Hoody" Hards helped in multiple ways; Sarah Olson helped collect many of the recent photographs; Scott DW Smith, of Imagesmith Photography, shot a great number of those photographs; and Gloryann Linch coordinated meetings.

At the Center of Southwest Studies, archives manager Nik Kendziorski located, scanned, and uploaded photos with George Usinowicz. Center staffers Julie Tapley-Booth, Jeanne Brako, Michael Long, Jen Pack, and the Center's doctoral fellow Joshua Salyers all gave support, as did Center interns and work-study students Andy Barrish and Georgie Pongyevsa.

San Juan National Forest recreation staff officer Jed Botsford provided access to historical documents known as "the Purgatory box" in the Columbine Ranger District office. Forest archaeologist Julie Coleman provided materials for a digitization project funded in part by the San Juan Mountains Association that proved timely for early San Juan Mountains history.

Editor Elizabeth Green refined material from all the contributing writers into the story you are about to read. Designer Lisa Snider created a vibrant layout featuring Purgatory's people, events, and landscape. Such roles as theirs bear the brunt of last-minute changes and pressures, and they handled all of those well, while making this a better book.

To all these, we say thank you for your help and encouragement along the way.

"The mystery of a mountain is extremely important. People come back year after year because of a mountain's mystery."

**- Paul Folwell,
trail designer and ski patrolman**

Mountain Paradise

A perfect place for skiing

For fifty years now, skiers have been cruising down the slopes of Purgatory Ski Area, enjoying the magnificent views, pristine powder, and towering forests.

Almost every geological force this planet has endured has played a part in creating this glorious landscape set in the San Juan National Forest. An ice field 1,000 feet thick massed over these mountains, leaving only the highest peaks projecting above its surface. Before that, volcanoes spewed ash and lava, swelling and cracking overlying layers of sediment while burying others. For 300 million years, ancient oceans rose and fell, leaving behind colorful layers of shale, limestone, and sandstone on the landscape.

Purgatory comprises 612 acres of deeded land and 2,500 acres of leased national forest land. Ski runs extend up in elevation from 8,793 feet at the base to over 10,822 feet at the top of the mountains.

Directly across from the resort can be seen the Twilight Peaks, carved from metamorphic gneiss 1.78 billion years old, and just south, the Needle Mountains, sculpted by glaciers from igneous granite 1.46 billion years old, some of the oldest rock in the Rockies. Pigeon Peak in the Needles is 13,972 feet high. Engineer Mountain's distinct profile to the north includes layers of marine-fossil-rich limestone topped by igneous rock. Hidden from view is 14,084-foot Eolus Peak, one of five "fourteeners" proximate to Purgatory, some of the highest peaks in the Rockies.

Early records attest to the use of the forest for eons by native peoples, including the Ute bands who valued these mountains as a haven, hunting ground, and place of spiritual importance. One early Forest Service document from Bayfield, Colorado, recalls an event in which one Ute band set these forests on fire while fleeing from a skirmish with a competing band high in the

Purgatory Resort

San Juans.

Anglo prospectors and settlers coming into the area beginning in the 1860s clashed with the Utes, leading to a series of treaties, including the Brunot agreement of 1873-74. Thereafter, the area opened to mining towns and the railroad. Ranching was common up and down the Animas River and Purgatory and Hermosa creeks, the area that became Purgatory Ski Area. Ranching families knew the area around Purgatory Creek and the upper Harris Park area best, including the Swires, the Tinkers, and the Harris brothers, each family long established in the region before the coming of recreational skiing in the mid-twentieth century.

Creators of America's national forests never envisioned anything like this magnificent ski area. By the late 1800s, mountains throughout the West were being stripped of timber, leaving the landscape susceptible to devastating erosion, which in turn fouled the streams and rivers. Forest reserves were set aside to enforce managed resource use,

Preceding pages: A glorious glimpse of the Twilights.

Scott DW Smith

Facing page: Engineer Mountain is one of the most recognizable peaks in the San Juans.

The US Forest Service:
Conservation and recreation

As the nineteenth century drew to a close, the nation's natural resources were facing increasing pressures from competing interests. The time had come to more carefully monitor and control their use.

The first step had been the designation of forest reserves, but by 1905, Congress created the US Forest Service to manage all the resources on those reserves under the principle of multiple use. Unlike the Park Service, which would be created eleven years later, the Forest Service would allow timber cutting, mineral extraction, and livestock grazing, but all under forest rangers' watchful eyes.

Founding Director Gifford Pinchot envisioned the land being put to its highest and best use, including homes, farms, power plants, mills, hotels, and more. That included leasing land for vacation homes. To this day, such privately owned structures exist on Forest Service lands.

Pinchot did not anticipate a growing interest in recreational uses of public lands that would pit interests against one another. Some groups lobby for preservation of public lands in their natural state, while others want them open to unrestricted use.

In Colorado and other mountain states, recreational skiing emerged in the 1930s and exploded after World War II. By the 1950s and 1960s, the Forest Service embarked on a proactive approach, identifying areas that would be suitable for various forms of organized recreation.

As interest in building ski areas blossomed, the agency was ready.

Purgatory Resort

Purgatory Resort

including timber harvesting, mining, livestock grazing, and dispersed recreational activities such as fishing, hunting, and hiking.

The US Forest Service, created in 1905 to oversee those lands, eventually melded multiple forests into the San Juan National Forest in 1947.

The idea of developed recreation in the form of campgrounds, ski areas, and more had not occurred to the founders of the Forest Service. Later, in the 1920s and 1930s, new interest in alpine winter sports grew in the United States. As a result the Forest Service began to encourage exploration for sites within the national forests that could be

utilized for skiing. Following World War II, forest personnel identified a growing number of potential sites, especially in mountainous states like Colorado.

By 1965, as interest in skiing grew, the groundwork—geological, cultural, governmental, and recreational—had been laid. Land around Purgatory Creek became available, and the right people were poised to build a ski area.

Hermosa Park:
The famous back-side

Purgatory's famed back-side is named Hermosa Park after the creek that flows through the valley. Here, behind the resort's front face, numerous ski runs of increasing difficulty spread out across the mountain and funnel down to lifts 3 (Hermosa Park Express), 5 (Grizzly), and 8 (Legends). On a clear day, skiers standing in the lift lines can witness the beauty of what was once an active summer pasture on the Harris Ranch.

The Harris family acquired the 480-acre ranch in 1934 in the midst of the Great Depression. John E. Harris and his sons worked the ranch as a summertime high-country grazing area accommodating 300 or more head of cattle each year for the better part of four decades. At the time they acquired the ranch the property featured a log cabin (still standing today), two barns, saddles, bedrolls, and a chuck wagon. Horses and cattle came along with the deal. This ranch was first established as three separate, 160-acre homestead and ranching claims by Daniel Murnane and George and William Pearson. The first of the claims dated to 1893, though the buildings are older.

Local historians believe the original log cabin, built circa 1880, is one of the early toll stations on the Rockwood to Rico toll road. Enterprising developers built the toll road to provide a more direct connection between Animas City/Durango and Rico, with its surrounding mines. The road was made obsolete by completion of the Rio Grande Southern Railroad in 1891. Now restored by the US Forest Service and local partners, the cabin is opened occasionally for historical tours.

Hermosa Park and its surroundings were long home to other uses by locals. From up and down the Animas River valley, nineteenth-century hunters ranged into the park with its rich resources of deer, elk, bear, and other game animals. Hunting continues to this day. Hermosa Creek, now a protected watershed due to a recent act of Congress, has been a prime fishing venue for the same period of time, if not longer.

Durango locals who hunted and fished the area were accustomed to using the old logging roads that laced the hillsides and led up to the higher reaches of what are now Purgatory's ski trails. Timbering continued in Hermosa Park throughout the past century as the area was surrounded by National Forest lands and freeholdings, all of which were part of the timbering industry in the area.

After decades of ranching, the Harris brothers sold their Hermosa Park land—one of them reluctantly—to the Durango Ski Corporation at Ray Duncan's request. Much of the former ranch forms part of the ski area boundary on the south side of Hermosa Park, but the land was exchanged for other land on the front side of Purgatory in a land swap with the Forest Service in 1991.

This area, below where Lift 1 would be built, had already been partially cleared for utility lines before construction of Purgatory started.

The Swire cabin was
located in what
became the base area.
Prior to construction
of the ski area, the
cabin was dismantled
and moved to the
Animas Valley, where it
became an art gallery.

This early aerial reconnaissance photo shows the original base site. US Highway 550 is at lower right, with the US Forest Service road leading to what would become the parking area just above it.

WELCOME TO PURGATORY!

All of us who are associated with Purgatory hope your stay is both pleasant and successful. Let me tell you about Purgatory. We are celebrating our tenth year of operation. In that time we have built slowly and carefully. Our skier visits have increased from 28,000 the first year to this year when we will host 150,000 skiing visitors, besides yourselves. We are proud of our course record. We have some of the best skiers in the world working for us. They ski this way because Purgatory offers a continuous challenge to skiers of all abilities.

Hopefully, you will find this year's race equally challenging and enjoyable, and may the best skiers win.

Chet Anderson
General Manager & Secretary.

CHESTER "CHET" ANDERSON

Chester "Chet" Anderson knows the Rockies. He knows the Front Range. He knows the Western Slope. He tramped all over the San Juans looking for an ideal ski area—and finally found Purgatory.

Before coming to Durango, Chet had been a US Forest Service snow ranger on the Front Range. In the San Juans, he continued searching for potential ski areas and skied the terrain to be sure. He knew easy access was essential for a ski area, as were vertical drop—at least 1,000 feet—availability of private land for commercial development, and room to expand. By 1963, he had settled on an area north of Durango, adjacent to US Highway 550.

Even before the local push for a ski area had gained traction, the Forest Service had agreed with him and identified the area that would become Purgatory.

Two years later, Purgatory founder Ray Duncan lured Chet away from the Forest Service to help "lay out the mountain." With snow still on the ground in the spring of 1965, he started identifying trails on snowshoes.

Using contour maps and aerial photos, he was able to envision the entire layout. "But the details were done in my head in the summer," he says, explaining that ski feasibility work is done when there is no snow.

"The only place it comes through is in your head. You can't put it on maps. You can't put it on photos . . . until you get it on the ground. And that's all summer work," he said, adding, "You have to walk the whole thing."

Chet was able to tell where the swamps and rocks were as well as where roads were, and weren't. It was important, too, that he could tell where he was at any moment, and how he could get from there to any other place on the mountain. With several benches traversing the mountain, it was easy to get confused, especially in dense timber.

"Every time I'd come on a bench, I'd ask myself, 'have I been on this bench before?'" Chet recalled years later. Trails had to be interconnected, and those connections could only be determined when the ground was bare.

"You can't do it on skis in the winter," he said. "Sure, you can check on wind, you can check on snow, but you can't envision skiing very well because you're too busy dodging trees to pay attention."

Chet enjoyed the challenge, and his determination paid off when he discovered a route to the bottom that novice skiers could use. Mountain planning was, quite simply, "fun" for him.

"It's really time-consuming. It's a big challenge, too. But it's tremendously creative," he said. "It's just as creative a process as . . . photography . . . or painting."

"You just have to have a feel that you can transpose what you're walking on and know it will ski."
– Chet Anderson

The Early Years

As a community rallies a ski resort is born

People have been skiing in the San Juan Mountains for more than a century. In the early days, it was hard work, accomplished on rudimentary equipment.

Mail carriers needed skis in the winter to carry mail from one mountain settlement to another. Miners got to high altitude mining camps on "snowshoes," which were actually long wooden skis. Linemen in the high country sometimes relied on skis to patrol the electric transmission lines from Tacoma power plant to mines, plants, and towns in winter. Mining tramways created the model for lifts that would later take skiers up the mountains.

Serious recreational alpine skiing in North America began in the 1930s when the first ski tows were built by local ski clubs and other enthusiasts. The 1932 Winter Olympics in Lake Placid and the 1936 winter games in Garmisch, where alpine ski races were first held, captured Americans' attention.

The first rope tows in North America (Shawbridge, Quebec, in 1933 and Gilbert's Hill in Vermont in 1934) were soon followed by the first rope tows in Colorado. Local skiers with some mechanical ability modified car and truck engines to power rope tows, and they organized local ski clubs to raise money for gas and other expenses to keep the tows operating.

A group of local skiers, including Walt Balliger, Jack Lee, Fred Klatt Sr., Bill Crawley, and Gerry and Dick Yeager, installed the Durango-area's first documented rope tow in Cascade Meadows on the flanks of Engineer Mountain in 1936-37. Two years later, they moved the tow south to Lechner Field, also known as Chipmunk Hill. With the onset of World War II, the tow was moved into Durango and installed at what later became known as Chapman Hill.

Following the war, folks increasingly came to see skiing as a challenging and fun winter sport for individuals and families. By the early 1960s, Southwest Colorado boasted several small ski areas with surface lifts, including Wolf Creek, Stoner, Hesperus, and Kendall Mountain. Dolph Kuss had replaced Third Avenue's (now Chapman Hill) old tow with one from the Tenth Mountain Division's Camp Hale in the mid-1950s. Cars provided an alternative to tows in the high country for ski runs like the power line on Coal Bank Hill.

As interest in the sport grew, people wanted more—more trails, more vertical drop, more

Top: Ray Duncan (left) and Chet Anderson (right) first began scouring the San Juans for potential ski areas in 1961. Here Duncan and Anderson are accompanied by Friedl Pfeifer (center), former resort planner at Aspen.

Bottom: Pfeifer, left, and Duncan survey the mountainside.

access, more amenities. Historian William Philpott noted in *Vacationland: Tourism and Environment in the Colorado High Country*, that people were seeking "a land where you could realize yourself by indulging your adventurous side and achieving inner peace." Moreover, skiing offered the allure of an exhilarating activity that families could share in the midst of a beautiful landscape.

Through the late 1950s and early 1960s, booming oil and gas development brought a surge of new residents to Durango, people with experiences and expectations that would fundamentally change their new hometown. Among these new arrivals was Ray Duncan, a young oilman who loved skiing and sought out those who felt the same way. He found several like-minded people who shared his enthusiasm, and together they founded Durango Ski Corporation in early 1965. They had two objectives: identify land that would be suitable for developing a major ski area and obtain the financing to build that ski area. He had a kindred spirit in Chet Anderson.

After arriving on the San Juan National Forest

Raymond T. Duncan wasn't much of a skier when he moved to Durango in 1958. But he was learning, and wanted to progress beyond snowplows and stem christies. For that, he wanted a ski area, a big one.

Ray checked out a number of places in the West before choosing Durango and opening his oil company's office in the West Building. He had moved to the right place at the right time. And his ability to motivate people and make things happen was about to bring the biggest change Durango had seen since the arrival of the railroad back in 1881.

He had taken up skiing two years earlier, in Aspen, and saw it as a wholesome, exhilarating family activity. In Durango, he found many people who shared that belief. Like him, they yearned for a bigger and better area to ski.

RAYMOND T. DUNCAN

It was Ray's entrepreneurial spirit, his ability to motivate people that helped make Purgatory ski area a reality. Chet Anderson, the original mountain manager, said Ray made people "a part of it . . . at least psychologically," adding that motivation "has a lot to do with the history of Purgatory."

Talk with employees who worked for and with Ray at Purgatory, and certain words are repeated over and over: *esprit de corps*, family, spirit, vision, camaraderie. "Ray Duncan felt responsible for his people at Purgatory," said Karen Malouff, his former director of personnel. In turn, she added, they "took on a real personal responsibility."

Ray was able to convince a group of Durango's most influential citizens that a ski area in the vicinity would be a good thing for the community as a whole. To the mayor, fellow business owners, and his employees, Ray's enthusiasm and caring for Durango and the surrounding area were infectious. His drive inspired them to be a part of his audacious plan.

Dolph Kuss, an avid skier and ski coach, was particularly pleased that Ray had moved to Durango. The two men shared a strong commitment to community, a desire to serve. "Ray maintained this sense of community," Dolph recalled. "He was altruistic in his feelings. I don't know if he ever thought about being concerned about making money."

Even after Ray moved his office to Denver in 1968, he remained closely involved with the ski area. Ruel "Major" Lefebvre, who was trail maintenance manager, stressed that things continued to run well after Ray's move because he had assembled an excellent team that included "some of the most qualified individuals that he could ever have on his staff."

Community confidence in Raymond T. Duncan and his vision earned him the Durango Chamber of Commerce Man of the Year award in January 1966, the premiere season of the newly created Purgatory Ski Area. Ray was inducted into the Colorado Ski Hall of Fame in 2006.

in the early 1960s, Chet had worked his way through much of the San Juan region considering peak and face one after another. He scouted Molas Pass, a site very much like some other existing pass ski areas (now a locals' favorite for backcountry skiing and high elevation cross-country skiing). The seasoned snow ranger considered slopes on the mountains surrounding Silverton, just twenty miles north of Purgatory. But each of these sites had limitations that ruled them out.

Chet, Ray, and their scouting partners agreed on their preferred site on US Highway 550, overlooking the Twilight Peaks and Spud Mountain, just twenty-five miles north of Durango. They decided to name the project "Purgatory" after the creek that flowed through the proposed base area. Chet went to work for Durango Ski Corporation as manager of Purgatory Ski Area on February 15, 1965, just twelve days after Forest Supervisor R. K. "Rod" Blacker accepted their feasibility study and gave the go-ahead for Ray's special use permit.

As local supporter and avid skier Bob Beers recounted, "A number of us got together and put in a thousand dollars each to form the nucleus of the company. . . . We then undertook to sell stock up and down Main Avenue." With that, they were able to secure a $350,000 Small Business Administration loan. Ray and his peers were able to raise the necessary funds in only thirty-eight days.

The initial master plan envisioned three phases of ski area development. The first phase included a single aerial tramway or lift, a T-bar, a base day lodge, and several ski trails on the front side. Two other phases envisioned mountain improvements expanding to the west as—and if—the ski area continued to grow. The team envisioned a mix of fifteen percent beginner runs, sixty percent intermediate slopes, and up to twenty-five percent advanced runs. The feasibility report noted that the ratios matched current ski industry averages for

the Western mountains.

Founders counted on Purgatory developing as a local-serving ski area while also drawing skiers from as far away as Phoenix and Albuquerque. To bolster the argument that the local market mattered, the feasibility report cited the very active Durango Ski Club, third largest in the state at the time despite its meager local facilities. Both the Durango High School and Fort Lewis College ski programs made it into the argument also. Though Fort Lewis College enrolled only 1,150 students at the time of writing, the author claimed that the college projected enrollment would triple in just five years. This sort of claim was important since the college had just hired Adolph "Dolph" Kuss, the coach of the 1964 U.S. Winter Olympic team and a ten-year Durango resident, to develop its intercollegiate ski team. The results of that hire were spectacular and tied directly to the development of the ski racing program at Purgatory.

Chet was the perfect man for the job of laying out Purgatory. He and Ray immediately began hiring their first employees. Ray recruited Jim

Top left: Cable is installed for Lift 1, known as Spud Mountain Lift.

Courtesy Keith Blackburn family

Above: A crane is used to install a tower for Lift 1.

Courtesy Keith Blackburn family

Marvin Dunagan had three unique claims to fame in the story of Purgatory's beginning. He was the first person hired by Chet Anderson, taking the jobs of maintenance manager and chief of lift operations. Marvin also wielded the first shovel of dirt for construction of Lift 1, a familiar undertaking for the man who had helped erect tows at Herperus ski area.

It also could be said that Marvin, his wife Joella, and their three sons were the "first family" of Purgatory. They moved onto the premises in a trailer in the spring of 1965 and lived there for three years.

"There wasn't anybody else around there then," said Marvin.

That fall Joella started commuting to the West Building in Durango, where she was in charge of ticket sales for Purgatory's opening season. The boys took the bus to school. After the Day Lodge was built, the kids all helped in the restaurant, waiting tables and cleaning restrooms.

Of course, the kids skied every chance they got, often coached by Chet Anderson, as they had been at Hesperus. Eventually Randy, the eldest son, became a ski patrolman.

Marvin assisted Earl Eaton of Eaton Manufacturing in building Lift 1. They faced tough working conditions, from deep snow—eight and a half inches on the upper lift station on June 1—and then more than three months of daily rain. No one thought the lift could be completed on time.

Marvin Dunagan, far right, stands with Chet Anderson, general manager, center, and Jim Morton, ski instructor, at opening day ceremonies.

The crew—including Earl Eaton, Chet Anderson, Bernie and Benny Basham, and some college kids, the Matis boys, Greg Fryback—did it all by themselves. The work was hard, too. With no helicopter to help move equipment and supplies, they had to pull small concrete mixers up and down the mountain with a bulldozer, more commonly referred to as a Cat.

Marvin enjoyed the cooperation among crew members, with everyone doing whatever was necessary to build the chairlift. Whether it was wielding chain saws or driving the Cat, people pitched in. It could be dangerous work, too, so the sound of "fire in the hole" made everyone duck for cover.

Marvin recalled an incident when he was driving the Cat.

> I flipped it over backwards on Demon, on that steep drop-off. I'd run it up as far as I could run it and let the blade down . . . let it come down slow, and back-drag the dirt down. . . . Well, while I was running it up, it climbed a green stump and went over backward. I just pushed myself out of it, jumped out, and landed where my glasses were. . . . It split my head from one end to the other.

Camaraderie, that word so often used to describe the spirit of those who built Purgatory, certainly helped Marvin and his crew get the job done. "Each one of us knowing each other as well as we did," he reflected, "that probably helped."

Helmericks—the owner of Telluride Iron works and a key figure in the creation of Bodo Industrial Park—to be the supervising engineer of the Purgatory project. Chet hired Marvin Dunagan, a Hesperus businessman who had helped install the ski tows at Hesperus ski area, as Purgatory's first maintenance manager.

Keith Blackburn, a mine worker from Telluride and former employee of Telluride Iron, came on as lift supervisor and helped with cables and tramways. Paul Folwell, a seasoned ski patrolman at Loveland ski area on the Front Range, assumed duties as the first ski patrolman at Purgatory and worked with Chet to design and lay out the trail system at the resort. Paul's wife, Sally Folwell, herself a ski instructor at Loveland and Arapahoe Basin, started out running the ticket office and rental shop while also teaching skiing part-time. She went on to develop Purgatory's personnel department over the course of several years before becoming Ray's administrative assistant. The Folwells divorced, and Sally later married Ray Duncan.

Bob Jacobson was recruited in July to organize and direct the Purgatory Ski School. He was a local who ranched and had taught skiing at Vail and Alta, Utah. He hired Jim Morton, from Winter Park, and Reiden Steinnes, a young Norwegian woman from the Snow Bowl in Flagstaff as ski instructors, and later added several part-time instructors. Dick Elder, owner of the Colorado Trails Ranch outside Durango, agreed to supervise Purgatory's construction and manage the lodge and restaurant at Purgatory.

These first employees developed a powerful camaraderie, sharing with the community an eager desire to create a local ski area and fulfill the founders' dreams.

From its first season beginning in December 1965, Purgatory steadily grew its base of operations, its trails, and its skier visits over the next decade.

Despite three months of daily rain and mud, Lift 1 was completed in time for opening day. The towers remained red for years, then were painted forest green.

Paul Folwell was always fascinated with ski trails. Perhaps it was his artist's eye that drew him to the curve and sweep of a trail, the design of a ski area, the planning of it all.

Paul has always had two loves: skiing and painting. And as is true for most artists, painting didn't pay the bills. But skiing did. He was a ski patrolman at Loveland when he heard about Ray Duncan and Chet Anderson's plans for a new ski area in the San Juan Mountains. He and his wife signed on to be a part of the venture.

Paul and Chet started envisioning the trail system long before anyone was ready to commit to putting in lifts. Chet was immediately impressed with how the young man could picture the entire mountain trail system in his mind. Fortunately for Purgatory, their ideas meshed.

Paul believed that trails had to do more than offer great skiing. They had to look good. It was a "revolutionary" approach, Paul recalled as he described the tree islands and feathered edges that distinguish Purgatory trails. He wanted people to feel they were skiing through meadows and forests, not just following clear-cut trails down the mountain. That was how to make Purgatory a memorable experience for everyone in the family.

It was, he stressed, "extremely difficult" to do, but vital for attracting repeat skiers. "Every time they come back they come across something they haven't skied before." That meant offering a variety of trails, some wide, others narrow chutes, still others glade trails, and what Paul calls "radical terrain changes."

PAUL FOLLWELL

Skiers have been enjoying the results of their collaboration for fifty years. "Trail design makes Purgatory unique," said Paul. "This is why Purgatory is one of the great ski mountains around."

As a landscape painter, Paul brought an artistic sensibilty to the mountains. Perhaps that's why he had such a good ability to envision a mountain plan and lay out the trails.

Not all of his mountain plans worked out, however.

Paul and Chet devised a grand plan for the north side of Hermosa Park, for instance—gondolas, thousand-foot lifts, a variety of spectacular runs, and some radical terrain—that never became reality because of changing environmental regulations. Nevertheless, one of the runs he envisioned, the one he calls "Ina," he painted just as he envisioned it.

It's not difficult to imagine the roar of chain saws as Paul laid down his brush strokes on the canvas. You're struck by the juxtaposition of light and shadows in the spruce, startled by the crisp bite of an axe as you follow the slash of white snow down the slope. A hint of yellow-ochre islands appears in the foreground, giving way to blue-grays and you note the feathered edges, selected trees brushed out.

This is what a ski run should look like.

"Ina" by Paul Folwell

The Day Lodge takes shape in the base area, while Lift 1 is completed above it.

Robert W. (George) Smith

Courtesy Marvin Dunagan family

Ray Duncan addresses the crowd on opening day.

Dean & Nancy Furry

Dean & Nancy Furry

Dick Elder, owner of the Colorado Trails Ranch, was hired to supervise construction of the Day Lodge. He and his wife Dolly managed the lodge, serving meals prepared by by chef Ming Wong and legendary pecan pies made by Maxine Thompson.

**Above: An early
photo of Lift 1 on the
left, and a Poma
surface lift
on the right.**

As coach of the Fort Lewis College ski team, **Adolph "Dolph" Kuss** was known as "Little Napoleon." Discipline was one of the traits that helped Dolph maintain an intercollegiate skiing program that was not only a national power, but also sent representatives to the Olympics as successful international competitors.

Tough conditioning, calisthenics, and ten-mile runs were parts of the program, of course, but Dolph also had the whole ski team working at Purgatory on the weekends breaking rock, filling sand bags, clearing trail, and piling brush. "If you needed something done on the spot, shoveling snow off the parking lot," for example, said Paul Folwell, who was mountain planner and ski patrolman at Purgatory, "you could always depend on Dolph's kids. . . . They were hard workers."

Although this kind of "volunteer" work was mandatory for the team, there were some rewards, including complimentary ski passes. Unlimited season passes from Durango Ski Corporation, noted Dolph, made it possible for them to have "one of the best programs in the United States."

Respect for discipline and hard work were not the only personality traits Dolph exhibited. As national gelande champion "Dirty" Don Hinkley acknowledged, people were expected to work hard if they wanted to make the team. Yet giving "an ounce" of effort prompted "a pound back" from coach Kuss.

Dolph was modest, though, insisting he'd rather have a pack of gum than a trophy because, "I can chew gum." What Dolph most enjoyed was seeing his skiers' names in the newspaper.

ADOLPH "DOLPH" KUSS

Dirty said the ski program benefitted Fort Lewis College by attracting new students from a wide area. The success could be measured on Tuesdays and Thursdays, when the campus virtually emptied out for "unbelievably large" ski classes.

Dolph gives much of the credit for the promotion of skiing in the community and the eventual development of Purgatory to Ray Duncan. The ski area founder, he said, wanted to "bring some attention to the area and the community and make better citizens."

Modesty aside, Dolph could be described as a coach for the community. In 1954, when he was hired as La Plata County recreation director, Dolph organized a year-round recreation program with an emphasis on skiing, developing young people in the community into fiercely competitive skiers.

And later, in the spring of 1965, when he teamed up with Ray and the Durango Ski Corporation, he stressed the importance of programs for young people and their value for the community. "Provide for the young people," he explained, and "they'll grow up and ski."

For all of his contributions—to Fort Lewis College, the

Dolph Kuss, third from left, poses with his Fort Lewis College ski team.

community of Durango, and Purgatory Ski Area—Coach Dolph Kuss was named to the Colorado Ski Hall of Fame.

The Clark and Hogan Families:
Devotees from the get-go

Purgatory had diehard fans even before it opened for business.

Prior to 1965, Durangoans were willing to go a long way to satisfy their thirst for skiing: Hesperus, Silverton, Stoner, Monarch, even Aspen. It was, Durango businessman H. Jackson Clark admitted, a "long haul."

There was no lack of ideas when avid skiers talked about where a local ski area might be built. So as word spread about plans for a new ski area close to Durango, folks were eager to check it out.

Jackson, his wife Mary Jane, and friends Mike Elliott, Dolph Kuss, and Mickey Hogan were on their way to ski Molas Pass in the spring of 1965 when heavy snow moved in. They decided instead to stop where Purgatory was about to be built. Thanks to old logging roads, they were able to drive partway up, then cross-country ski to the top of the mountain before racing to the bottom.

Mary Jane and Antonia Clark.

Throughout that snowy spring, they continued to ski in the area, sometimes joined by other friends. The snow was, Mickey recalled, "excellent."

When Purgatory opened, Mickey and Maureen Hogan bought the first season tickets for themselves and their four young children. Many other families followed suit. The Clarks skied Purgatory more than a dozen times that winter and found their children could ski the mountain from top to bottom.

Most of the families went through Purgatory's ski school at one time or another. Ladies quickly formed the Wednesday Ladies Club, which Charlie Langdon dubbed "the longest running party in the region" in his book *Durango Ski*. The Men's Friday Club followed soon afterward.

All in all, though, skiing at Purgatory was and remains a family affair. Generations of families like the Hogans and the Clarks have continued the traditions that started that first season fifty years ago.

Jackson Clark's daughter Antonia was twelve when Purgatory opened and her brother Jackson, known as J.C., was fourteen. They would hitch a ride to the ski area with anyone who was headed up to the mountain. And whenever their mother went, Antonia and her friends went along—even if it meant sneaking out of school.

As the result of such shenanigans, the truant officer sometimes went to the ski area and stood at the base of the lift, watching for hooky-playing students. J.C. recalls a day when the principal actually joined them in line.

By his junior year of high school, J.C. started teaching in the Purgatory ski school. In that same year, Antonia was ski racing, winning the state high school championship in the giant slalom.

Families from near and far keep coming. Whatever brings them back—the mixture of terrain, or the sunny days and mild winters, or the sheer beauty of the setting—they, like the Clarks and Hogans, have made Purgatory *their* ski area.

Ski school director Bob Jacobson stands ready to welcome you to a winter of fun on the Purgatory slopes.

Learning to ski?
Want to ski better?
This is THE year!

Purgatory has groomed the slopes and staffed its school with the finest instructors anywhere to make this year a ski year for you. There's a class for everyone so . . . join the fun!

LADIES' DAY — Wednesday, featuring the feminine approach to the slopes

MEN'S DAY — Friday, a day the perfect finish to the busine

FT. LEWIS DAYS — Tuesday, college oriented from Schussers

YOUNGSTERS' DAYS — Sunday, focusing on you needs from beginners to ra by the ski school with Ol Meyers

Make this a fun year
Buy season tickets now — son of ski fun. Call or wr West Building, Durango,

Volunteer ski
patrolmen practiced
on-slope toboggan
rescues and chairlift
evacuations during the
first season.

Trails were groomed
with a combination of
equipment like these
Tucker snowcats and
by volunteers who
sidestepped down the
mountain packing
snow.

David Camp does a
front flip with Twilight
Peaks in the back-
ground, in 1975.

Eric Hodges

Facing page:
Purgatory hosted
national men's and
women's
championships,
including events in
cross-country, alpine,
and gelande jumping.
Here, a gelande
jumper soars over
Catharsis.

Paul Souder

"Purgatory has the best all-around ski conditions and snow conditions in the country. We don't get a lot of deep powder but we always have a good pack. I've never seen ice up here."
– Bob Jacobson
Ski School director

Rejuvenation of Durango

Transformed to a year-round tourist town

For centuries before the first white explorers ventured into the San Juan Mountains, Ute Indians had hunted there, wearing deep tracks through their Shining Mountains. But no one stayed in the mountains year-round—at least not until gold was discovered. The glitter proved irresistible, and before long, prospectors were probing every nook and crease.

Founded in 1880 by the Denver & Rio Grande Railway, Durango became the supply depot and smelting center for gold and silver mines in the surrounding area. From its inception, and even more by 1882, when the railroad to Silverton was completed, Durango was a western boomtown.

Mining and smelting of precious metals were the backbone of the town's economy, along with agriculture, which provided the food and livestock that couldn't be grown in the high country. Durango experienced some difficult setbacks through the years. A catastrophic fire in 1889 wiped out a big portion of the business district as well as homes, churches, and town offices. The repeal of the Sherman Silver Purchase Act dealt another blow in 1893, as did labor strikes in 1899 and 1902 and a massive flood in 1911. Nonetheless, Durango survived.

By the 1950s, mining had declined, and except for a short-lived uranium boom, the town had to look elsewhere for its livelihood. Summer brought tourists eager to see the mountains and nearby Mesa Verde National Park. But in winter, the town practically rolled up its proverbial sidewalks. Then came the oil and gas boom and with it, an increase in population and home building.

Around that time, people were starting to look beyond an economy

Preceding page:
Ski instructor J.C. Clark skis through pristine powder in the backcountry.
Robert W. (George) Smith

Facing page:
Ski patrolman Milt "Coyote" Wiley skis the trees in deep powder.
Robert W. (George) Smith

What's in a name:
Tracing history by the trails

Skiers can tell a little bit about Purgatory's history just by reading trail names. On the front of the mountain, names for the first trails were inspired by—although not all derived directly from—Dante's *The Divine Comedy*: Styx, Pandemonium, Inferno, Paradise, Catharsis, Hades, Demon, Pitchfork, El Diablo, and Limbo. One trail off Catharsis was originally called 666—the number of the beast in Revelations—but Vince Duncan objected to the name and it was changed to No Mercy in about 1990. (At the same time, Vince had the ski area's address changed from Box 666 to #1 Skier Place.)

The times, they were a-changing as trails were developed to the west, and the names reflect the Age of Aquarius: Peace, Boogie, Nirvana, Cool It, Divinity, Path to Peace, Salvation, Angels' Tread, Poets Glade, and Cathedral Treeway.

On the back side, known as Legends, names were earned by people who are legendary in Purgatory's history: Ray's Ridge and Zinfandel for Ray Duncan (he was getting into the wine business at the time), Vincent's for his older brother, and Sally's Run for his wife. Blackburn Bash is for Keith Blackburn and Benny Basham, while Paul's Park is for Paul Folwell, and Chet's is for Chet Anderson. The list goes on: Boudreaux's, Elliott's, Siegele Street, Bottom's Chute, Hoody's, and McCormack's Maze.

based on minerals and fuels, recognizing that scenery and climate could be equally valuable. Set in the beautiful San Juan Mountains and imbued with the history and culture of the Old West, Durango was well positioned to take advantage of the new trend. The creation of Purgatory Ski Area could not have been timed better.

People flocked to the town and its nearby ski

Adaptive Sports
Overcoming disability barriers

In 1971, Skip Merry, a part-time instructor in Purgatory's ski school, faced a new challenge he wasn't sure he could conquer: a blind woman wanted to ski.

Through trial and error, he developed a tactic that came to be known as the "Merry Method." With the blind skier holding one end of a pole and Merry holding the other, the two skied side-by-side. By pushing the pole left or right, Merry could guide the skier through turns. With practice, the blind skier learned to sense the fall line and could ski without the pole.

Merry taught his method to other instructors—Gene Roberts, Mike Piccoli, and Jackson Clark, among them—by first getting them used to being blind. He taught them how to get on and off chairlifts and ski down the slopes, all while blindfolded. Roberts took over the program when Merry left in the late 1970s, but after he also left, the program languished—until the irrepressible Dave Spencer revived it. As a cancer survivor with only one leg, Spencer knew what learning to ski had done for him.

In 1983, Spencer and Joe Wilson formed the nonprofit Durango Purgatory Handicapped Sports and broadened the program to include many disabilities in addition to blindness. Although it was a separate entity, the program received great support—financial and otherwise—from the ski area.

John Koca, disabled since age thirteen, first started skiing at Purgatory in 1977, on a ski he designed and made himself from a plywood platform and harness attached to a wooden ski. Purgatory personnel from the ski rental and maintenance shops fashioned a new ski for Koca using broken skis, and shortened his ski poles to an appropriate length for his use. With instruction from Gene Roberts, Koca was soon avidly skiing in standard races on Purgatory's slopes, and even earned an award as "Best Performance on a Single Ski" in the giant slalom.

Top: John Koca competes on his hand-made mono-ski.

Tony Schweikle

Below: Skip Merry uses his ski pole to guide a blind skier.

In the late 1980s, Spencer and Wilson organized a four-day ski racing event which paired National Football League players with disabled skiers, sponsored by Purgatory. The event not only raised money for the program, but also demonstrated that people with disabilities could learn to ski.

By that time in a single season, some 350 disabled skiers were taught by ninety volunteer instructors at Purgatory. Skier-days for the disabled totaled more than 1,300.

Durango Purgatory Handicapped Sports later became Adaptive Sports Association, and branched out to include many other outdoor pursuits that were once unavailable to people with disabilities. It remains a vital part of Purgatory's community outreach.

**Ski School director
Fritz Tatzer, right,
gives lift instructions
to skiers.**

Dean & Nancy Furry

area. By its fifth year, a second lift (Engineer) was in operation and Purgatory welcomed an impressive 50,000 skiers for what proved to be its longest season yet, 138 days. With completion of the original Powderhouse, skiers could stay up on the mountain all day. In town, from gas stations to hotels, and restaurants to stores, businesses were feeling the benefits of winter tourism.

Of course, from the very beginning, there were naysayers who complained about outsiders spoiling "their" town. They accused the ski area of destroying Durango's small-town character. They lamented that development—from the oil and gas boom as well as the ski area—was making Durango too urban. Construction of two glass and steel buildings, a notable departure from the city's much vaunted Victorian architecture, only seemed to reinforce the concerns.

People worried that tourism was an unreliable base for the economy, that it would foster low-paying jobs and undermine Durango's traditional roots of ranching, farming, and mining. There were complaints, too, that Purgatory didn't do enough to take care of locals, particularly some of those who had supported the ski area's initial development.

Despite the occasional grumbling, most embraced the ski area as it continued to grow—and Durango continued to thrive. In 1970, the Inn at Purgatory opened, followed by Twilight, East Rim, and Edelweiss condominiums in 1972. In 1976, the Twilight lift (Lift 4) was added. Good years outnumbered bad, as more and more skiers discovered the area that was gaining a reputation for abundant sunshine and great powder. The oil and gas embargo in 1973-74 took a huge bite out of attendance, but the next year proved to be Purgatory's best to date, with nearly 200,000 skiers and a record 490 inches of snow.

Summer attractions were added as well, with the Alpine Slide and Twilight Dinner Concerts at the Powderhouse in 1979. The following year, a fourth lift—Grizzly Peak (Lift 5)—was constructed.

Changes during the first fifteen years were soon to be dwarfed by a flurry of development in the 1980s. The ski corporation announced a ten-year plan, which was projected to cost as much as $250 million. Two new lifts—Needles (Lift 6), and Graduate (Lift 7)—came in 1982, along with

snowmaking on 100 acres and a second restaurant on the mountain. Dante's would be more upscale than the Powderhouse, with sit-down dining. The $9 million Village Center, with shops, restaurants, and high-end condominiums followed in 1983-84. The next year brought a $1.5 million water system, the $12 million Eolus Condominiums, the Kendall Mountain complex, and two more lifts. Beginners now had a separate area, with a second lift (Columbine, Lift 9) while skiable terrain on the mountain increased by twenty-five percent with the opening of the Legends area with its namesake Lift 8.

At the same time, development in the area surrounding Purgatory surged as well, with construction at Cascade Village to the north and Silver Pick, Needles, and Tamarron to the south. It was all a bit overwhelming to Durangoans.

Critics lamented that Purgatory was changing from a local ski area to a destination resort. They feared the planned hotels, condominiums, and restaurants would take money away from the town, as would real estate sales around the mountain. The newspaper reported that between 1982 and 1985, Purgatory had "increased in size forty percent." Locals complained, too, that the ski area's $1 million-a-year marketing program would attract more affluent skiers, detracting even further from its local flavor.

To at least some in the Durango business community, it seemed that the goose might be taking back its golden egg. In his defense of Purgatory's growth plan, Dick Peterson, president of the Durango Ski Corporation and CEO, explained that Purgatory was responding to changes in the ski market. "Our goal is to appeal to the families that hadn't previously come to Durango or Purgatory," he said, "the destination guest that planned ahead on his vacation, who will pay the price and stay at the slopes."

Ultimately, the controversy dwindled as locals realized what Deborah Uroda wrote in the *Durango Herald*: "If Purgatory doesn't provide the condos, then the ski area doesn't grow, and that doesn't help Durango."

In a recent interview, J.C. Clark recalled a story his father, one of the original investors, had told him.

> The average business guy could see what Purgatory would do for local businesses. My dad used to tell the story about going to see Woodrow Wong at the Western Steakhouse. … He just walked in there and Woodrow gave him a check for a thousand dollars. And they *did* get a return. They got the business. Mr. Wong didn't care about skiing, but he sure wanted people coming into his restaurant.

The Powderhouse opened for the 1969-70 season. Above, the Duncan family takes a break from skiing in the Powderhouse.

In 1978, Ray Duncan called in **Richard L. "Dick" Peterson**, one of the directors on the Durango Ski Corporation Board, to ask what he should do with Purgatory. He felt he had to make a choice: either keep Purgatory as a small ski area for locals or make it grow.

Duncan's decision came with a caveat, though. If he chose to make the resort grow, Dick would have to lead that growth.

The men had known one another for some time, so Ray was aware of Dick's abilities. The seasoned businessman was good at getting things done, managing big projects. He had been president of Vail Associates, and overseen big resort and residential construction jobs.

RICHARD L. "DICK" PETERSON

Dick saw an opportunity to improve on the way he had done things at Vail. He was being given the chance to transform complacent little Purgatory into a destination resort. So he gathered a small group of trusted co-workers from Vail and formulated a game plan. The main goal was to make Purgatory a high quality, family-friendly, service-oriented destination resort.

First, they had to concentrate on expanding the terrain, including creating a dedicated beginners area. They built new runs and lifts downhill from the base, in the Columbine area, giving new skiers a separate area to learn and practice their turns.

Later, in 1985-86, Lift 8 would be added, opening more intermediate/advanced terrain in the Legends area, then Lift 9, the second beginner's lift, opened at Columbine Station. They would also add Dante's restaurant, offering fine dining on the mountain.

Just as the resort needed more than new trails and lifts, it also needed additional overnight accommodations. Dick knew that more affluent skiers wanted to stay at the ski area so they could walk out the door and hit the slopes.

So in late 1978 through mid-1979, Dick's team drafted plans for significant new development at the base, including a showpiece village center building. In 1981 he was named CEO.

By 1989, (Dick's last year with the resort), Purgatory had not only built three significant base area buildings (the Village Center, Eolus, and Kendall) but also created its real estate company. The base village buildings dramatically changed the amenities and guest services available for destination and local guests.

In five years, they invested $50 million on the mountain, the lifts, new equipment, all the infrastructure ($1.5 million alone for a new water system), the Village Center and condominiums. Other new additions included a central reservations system, a medical clinic, the handicapped sports association, and improved training and benefits for their employees ($12 million in wages). During Dick's tenure as CEO, annual skier visits rose to more than 300,000.

But the changes that took place at Purgatory during those years were not without consequences. The workload had been tough, with building all summer and operating the resort all winter. Some employees became disgruntled by changing responsibilities and job descriptions.

Dick had pushed hard and expected a lot from people, but no one could downplay his immense accomplishments in a relatively short period of time.

**Purgatory employees
Mary Lou Murray, left,
and Julie Simmons,
pose for a poster.**

KIM MORTON & MARY LOU MURRAY

What does it take to make employees feel like a team, work hard, and have fun doing it? Just ask the people who have lived it.

Karen Bell, Carlyn Hodges, Kim Morton, and **Mary Lou Murray** filled a number of positions at the resort: personnel, marketing, ski school, guest services, accounting, virtually anywhere they were needed. If something needed doing, people stepped up and did it—like a team, they said.

It goes beyond their shared love of skiing. They are grateful for the opportunities they had at Purgatory, the chance to learn new skills, to advance to management positions, and to work with great mentors.

Purgatory had been in business for ten years when Karen arrived. She chose Durango because it was a ski town, and applied to be a ski instructor at Purgatory. Always encouraged and rewarded through her fifteen-year career there, she moved up the ranks to director of human resources. In the course of her journey, she found that "position status" didn't matter. Everyone worked hard and supported one another.

Karen eventually became CEO Dick Peterson's assistant, and remains especially grateful for the training and skill-building he fostered. She helped him create and run the "Rave Review" employee recognition program which rewarded employees for positive attitudes and actions.

Purgatory was ahead of its time in offering management opportunities for women, a trend that continues today. Karen particularly credits comptroller Bob Hill and chief financial officer John Ogier not only for supporting women employees, but also for creating a fun, people-friendly work environment.

Kim, a ski instructor who started the women's ski program in the 1980s, says Ogier and owner Ray Duncan fostered an open environment in which women were encouraged to excel. She did exactly that, creating a program for women teaching women to ski, which expanded nationally through the Professional Ski Instructors of America.

KAREN BELL

Skiers were always part of the equation as well, according to Kim, who stresses that Purgatory was "about the locals who skied there and loved it."

Like Karen, Carlyn worked in a variety of jobs, starting with the central cashier's office in 1980, and soon moved on to human resources. Sharing a very small office made employees in the department close, since they were "practically on top of each other." Duncan's generosity, Peterson's commitment to customer service, and Hill's support of women left strong impressions on her as she worked in guest services, central reservations, and marketing. Throughout the staff, there was a "sense of common purpose and a great love" for "their" ski area.

Mary Lou started in guest relations in 1985, but like the other women worked several different jobs, including central cashier, purchasing, cost accounting, guest relations, ticketing, group sales, activities, the host/hostess program, special programs, and more. She learned to ski at Purgatory—in part from Kim Morton—and relished the freedom to hit the slopes, even in the midst of a work day. Bob Hill "encouraged everyone to ski," she said, adding that she willingly stayed later to make up for the privilege.

All four women agree that working at Purgatory carried lifetime benefits for them: close friends, new skills, and an abiding love of skiing.

CARLYN HODGES

SKI
PURGATORY
THE COLORADO
CONNECTION

PURGATORY

1976-1977 Ski Season
Durango Chamber of Commerce Reservation Service

PURGATORY

PURGATORY RESORT
Durango, Colorado
'82-'83

'80-
DU

Paul Souder

Paul Souder

World class Olympic and professional skiers from France and the US pause at the top of Paradise during their training at Purgatory. From left, Guy Perillat, Chuck Ferries, Terry Palmer, Mike Lafferty, Jean Noel Augert, Tyler Palmer, and Jean-Claude Killy. Killy said the San Juans were "the most beautiful mountains outside of the Italian Alps."

Robert W. (George) Smith

Facing page: Lift 2, called Engineer after the mountain seen in the background, was built in 1969.

"We want to bring people into the community because we benefit too. . . . Whatever is good for Durango is good for Purgatory."

**- Mike Elliott,
marketing director**

Changes and Challenges

Economy and weather bring tough times

Purgatory grew rapidly through its first twenty years, adding seven more lifts and reaching 300,000 skier visits a year. The physical footprint of the mountain improvements extended towards the western boundary of the Forest Service permit area.

The resort was about to experience significant growing pains, and face tough questions about its future.

The first was in the base village, where rapid development of resort condominiums ran into the economic challenges of the Texas oil bust. Back in the 1970s, a scarcity of oil had kept skiers away. Now a sustained decline in demand led to increased unemployment, which significantly affected both winter and summer tourism. The resort was forced to cancel or scale back its base area development plans.

The construction of Lifts 8 and 9 was also delayed by several years because of the economic downturn. The resultant loss of revenues made it difficult for the resort to continue funding its growth via bond issues and created ongoing debt service issues that would challenge Purgatory for nearly a decade.

From an entirely different standpoint, a new trend in snow sports further challenged the ski area in the 1980s. Snowboarding was welcomed by some ski areas and shunned by others. Purgatory's mountain manager Bill Murphy was one of the few in the industry who embraced this new equipment early on. Initially, snowboarders had to get a special certificate from the ski school to document that they were qualified to ride their snowboards safely on the trails. Purgatory's first half-pipe was built in 1986 under Lift 2, and was known as the "Trick

Scott DW Smith

Ditch" for all the fantastic tricks that lift riders could witness. Ray Duncan's son Kevin opened the first snowboard shop in Durango, in the Village Center Building. And early representatives of the Burton and Sims snowboard companies came to Purgatory for frequent events and demonstrations.

Several back-to-back low snow years further strained the resort's finances, which were already thin due to the debt service levels from the prior growth period. By 1989, Dick Peterson moved on and CFO John Ogier took the helm. Ray Duncan was spending more and more time in California as his wine business took shape. And when the resort's line of credit was not renewed by a Denver Bank in the spring of 1990, all but three of the resort's employees were temporarily laid off. The resort searched for a solution and new ways to capitalize its future. John reached out to Ray's brother, Vince Duncan Sr. who helped him renegotiate the resort's debt and contributed more capital to help put the company back on firm footing.

At the same time, American attitudes toward the environment were changing. People became more concerned with conservation—at least in the places where they enjoyed leisure pursuits. As ski areas proliferated, the inevitable questions arose over how to accommodate demand for more skiing and summer recreational facilities without compromising the natural beauty and resources.

To be clear, the San Juan Mountains were not pristine forest. Significant mining had occurred between Silverton and Telluride to the north, and the Purgatory area was an important transport route for getting supplies to the high country and silver and gold to the Durango smelters. Extensive timber harvests were the norm, leaving numerous logging roads crisscrossing the terrain. Water from Cascade Creek was diverted to provide hydro power. Summer grazing of cattle was prevalent and locals fished and hunted the abundant wildlife.

From its inception, Purgatory Resort always maintained a cooperative partnership with forest resource managers and local environmental experts. Several of its early managers had worked with either the Forest Service or other ski resorts and understood the importance of thoughtful resource management. The Forest Service and Purgatory's management documented existing conditions and potential environmental impacts to the mountain, including utilizing existing roads as maintenance routes, relying in part on the existing Cascade aqueduct for snowmaking water supply, avoiding damage to sensitive wetland areas, and designing ski trails with feathered edges and tree islands.

As the ski area grew, there were many lessons learned by the new management team. Existing logging roads were removed or restored to their native condition to address erosion/sedimentation concerns from seasonally heavy rains and spring runoff. Special erosion control and re-vegetation

Environmental Ethos

Perhaps the greatest evidence of Purgatory's environmental ethos is its ability to continually improve its environmental processes and creatively partner/solve the challenges associated with building mountain improvements and base area development in sensitive high elevation environs.

Its "environmental stewardship" score from the Ski Area Citizens' Coalition is ample evidence of that commitment. This score ranks all ski areas in the nation by a comprehensive set of criteria across a wide spectrum of environmental issues—from habitat protection, to watershed protection, to addressing climate change, to environmental policies and practices. The scorecard generally favors those resorts that are built out and are not growing/building mountain and community improvements.

Accordingly, the resort began the last decade with a "D-minus" score, at the bottom of all Colorado resorts. Over the last fifteen years, however, the resort's initiatives and results have consistently improved its environmental score, ultimately earning an "A."

techniques were developed. The location of certain mountain improvements was adjusted to reduce impact. Culverts were installed on Purgatory Creek through the base area to preserve its water

JOHN OGIER

VINCENT DUNCAN

John Ogier's neat, tailored appearance hints at his profession as a financial officer. But his quiet, unflappable demeanor belies the challenges he faced during his years with Purgatory.

John was hired first as a consultant in 1983, charged with coordinating the merging of Purgatory Development Company with Durango Ski Corporation. Five years later, he was named executive vice-president and chief operating officer. One might aptly call him "chief juggler," as his duties included planning real estate and mountain development while balancing resort operations, aesthetics, and land values.

As such, he became the point man for a complex negotiation that extended through eight of his ten years with Purgatory. With changing priorities in the US Forest Service, the resort's original master plan calling for extensive development of the old Harris Ranch was dropped. His task was to find suitable properties to effect a trade with the Forest Service. After an exhaustive search, Ogier settled on first acquiring two additional parcels that were surrounded by Forest Service land, then bundling them with the 480-acre Harris Ranch property. They then exchanged the three parcels for nearly 500 acres of prime land along the highway corridor.

Meanwhile, Purgatory was facing new challenges. The real estate market declined sharply, particularly after new tax laws eliminated deductions for certain interest, depreciation, and appreciation expenses. People backed out of contracts for condominiums, and new buyers were almost nonexistent.

The Elk Point time-share project had to be abandoned. Deposits had to be refunded and Purgatory was unable to pay back the Industrial Development Revenue Bonds that had been used to finance the project. Negotiations to re-capitalize the bonds were tense, as it came down to Ray Duncan's personal guarantee.

The situation was dire, Ogier recalled. All the company's cash had been "drained off by real estate" and the bank refused to issue a line of credit.

"Things were in jeopardy," Ogier said. "When we weren't able to make payroll we had to lay off personnel, reducing their numbers to fifteen or twenty employees."

Finally, Ray's brother Vince stepped in. Already the second largest shareholder in the corporation, Vince guided John through negotiations with the bank. They were able to reissue the bonds and after six weeks, United Bank of Denver agreed to lend Purgatory money.

After John left the company, bondholders became concerned about the value of their investments. **Vince Duncan** stepped up and bought them out.

"Vince was a very honorable guy," John said.

What sets Purgatory apart, according to John, is the stakeholders, "the citizens of Durango, the employees, all of the contractors we've hired, our suppliers, our customers." Unlike other large ski areas, Purgatory has retained a sense of community. "The stakeholder concept—that's a vision that's been there from the start."

quality. Each of these actions involved environmental assessment and cooperative problem-solving with the resort's regulatory partners.

The Forest Service, nationally and regionally, was beginning to focus on a systemic approach to management plans for entire watersheds and ecosystems. As a result, Forest Service leaders and environmental groups considered the Hermosa Creek watershed important to manage as a whole. To accomplish this, they felt that Purgatory's private land in-holdings in Hermosa Park would have to be returned to public ownership.

The resort's original master plan had envisioned two distinct base villages on private land to provide residential, lodging, and commercial support for the ski operation. The front-side village (now known as Purgatory Village) was the smaller of the two, totaling about 100 acres. The larger back-side village was to be located on the old 480-acre Harris Ranch in Hermosa Park. In addition to base facilities near Lifts 3, 5, and 8, this Harris Ranch village would include a golf course and a series of retention ponds for golf course irrigation and water storage for snowmaking.

As the resort's lifts and ski trails expanded westward, and as the front-side village was further developed, resort management began to reassess the feasibility of developing the back-side village. After several years of environmental analysis and negotiations, in June 1990 the two parties concluded an agreement. The Harris Ranch lands and two other forest in-holdings acquired by the ski corporation—a total of 810 acres—would be given to the Forest Service in exchange for nearly 500 acres of Forest Service land east and west of US Highway 550 north, adjoining the existing front side of Purgatory Village.

With the land exchange complete, Vince Sr. and the Duncan family felt the resort needed new leadership, so they hired Vern Greco from Steamboat Resort in Northwest Colorado. Vern brought with him several Steamboat managers and began to implement numerous strategies that he thought were important to make Purgatory competitive with other Colorado resorts. He and the Purgatory team built the resort's first high-speed, detachable lift (Lift 3) in 1995. He implemented new software systems and uniforms/appearance standards and several other processes he had seen at other ski areas. But Vern's management style did not always fit with the culture that the Duncans had imbedded at Purgatory. And conflicts developed with many townsfolk as well. Vern left in 1998 for Park City, to lay the groundwork for the upcoming Olympic Games.

Throughout the 1990s, after several decades of service, the resort's original founding managers gradually began to retire or move on. This created a changing of the guard and the promotion of several staff members into a second generation of leaders.

Fortunately, virtually all of these new managers had learned management of the resort from the original generation and had worked for many years at the resort. So the resort's culture and legacy of family friendliness continued forward.

For many years, an in-house crew did all timber clearing – a dangerous job. Note two women on the crew in this photo.

RUEL "MAJOR" LEFEBVRE

Purgatory has had a multitude of "owners" through the years. There are the obvious ones, like Ray Duncan and Chuck Cobb, who have invested money in the resort. There are the locals who welcomed the ski area and have remained loyal through the years. And there are the people whose hard work and skills have made it the resort that it is.

Ruel "Major" Lefebvre is that kind of owner. As a trail maintenance manager, Major saw to it that everything worked as it should. It was never an easy job.

From operating equipment and teaching other people how to use it to scheduling daily trail maintenance in the winter, Major embraced his work with a sense of ownership.

"I look at the mountain." Major reflected, "and say 'that's my mountain.'"

Major initially went to work part-time at Purgatory, just enough to earn a season pass. As a successful competitor in nordic combined—ski jumping and cross-country skiing—he had been an alternate on the 1968 US Olympic team before coming to Colorado. Paul Folwell was so impressed by his work ethic that he persuaded the Vietnam veteran to stay.

It's hard to tell where his work day stopped and his recreational skiing started. Major helped determine the grooming schedules for the evening and graveyard shifts. Every morning he skied the runs, just to make sure everything had been done properly.

"I can do anything," he said in an interview years ago, listing all the equipment he could operate. "It's a lot of hard work, but it's all worth it to make Purgatory the best ski experience possible."

Major was known among his co-workers as the Yogi Berra of Purgatory for such expressions as "water over the bridge" and "six of one, dozen of the other." His notations on the maintenance schedules evoked laughter as well, since his "r's" often looked like "n's," making Swire Gulch into Swine Gulch. One issue of the ski patrol's irreverent comic strip, Zeke the Geek Comics, was devoted to his malapropisms and dubbed "The Book of Majorisms."

Yet while other employees past and present talk about relationships with their co-workers, Major was a bit different. His strongest working relationship was with the mountain itself. It was far more than rock and trees and snow to him.

"A ski area is a living thing," he said. And taking care of that living thing was Major's passion.

By his own admission, **Don "Boudreaux" Miller** was a ski bum. From the time he started skiing in his early teens, it was all he wanted to do. He figured if he could get a job skiing, he wouldn't have to stand in lift lines.

He got his first ski-town job in Aspen in 1954. Later, he and high school friend Paul Folwell were "kind of in the laundry and dry cleaning business" in Georgetown until Paul took a job at Purgatory. Boudreaux went to work at Arapahoe Basin as a ski patrolman and groomer.

In the summer of 1973, he visited Paul, who offered him a job driving snowcats at Purgatory. That job blossomed into a 30-year career, spanning the years from Ray Duncan and Chet Anderson to Chuck Cobb and Gary Derck. In his younger days, Boudreaux looked a little like Jerry Garcia, and his gruff demeanor inspired his radio nickname, "Grumpy Bear." But he got along well with the management and employees.

DON "BOUDREAUX" MILLER

As grooming supervisor and trail maintenance director Boudreaux was always looking for better ways to groom snow and improve the skiing experience. It was his idea, for example, to replace a single roller pulled behind a snowcat with three staggered rollers, called "gang rollers."

He and his crew had a sense of humor too, particularly when it came to the friendly rivalry between trail maintenance workers and ski patrolmen. Snow was quickly skied off the headwall break-overs on Purgatory's stair-stepped terrain and had to be replaced. In a process they dubbed bowling for "dinks" (their mocking term for patrolmen), a snowcat driver pushed snow over the headwall, while ski patrolmen and trail maintenance workers on skis below the headwall caught the snow and packed it down.

After disastrous snow droughts in 1976-77 and 1980-81, Purgatory decided to invest in snowmaking. Boudreaux and Herman Muhlbacher made the first artificial snow by hooking a diesel Headco to a fire hydrant at the base area. They covered an area about the size of four football fields, while also coating the Day Lodge deck and windows.

Boudreaux was in many ways an unsung hero in the expansion and improvement of Purgatory's trail system. As director of trails in his later years, he was responsible for all activities involving the trail system, winter and summer.

Boudreaux poses with Jack Turner.

He ended his career in 2003, and has since become "a successful, retired ski bum."

Preceding page:
A snowboarder makes
his way through
moguls on a front-side
black diamond trail.

Scott DW Smith photo

Above:
"Dirty" Don Hinkley
demonstrates gelande
jumping.

"Dirty" Don Hinkley was one of Dolph Kuss's boys. Coming to Durango from Vermont to join the Fort Lewis College ski team, Dirty went on to become the national amateur gelande champion in 1970, then national pro gelande champion and a member of Fort Lewis College's NCAA championship slalom team in 1972. Unlike in nordic ski jumping, gelande jumpers compete on alpine skiing equipment, which means the skier's entire foot is clamped to the ski, not just the toe.

After college, Dirty got a job at Purgatory and except for an eleven-year hiatus, has been there ever since. He became the trail construction supervisor in the 1970s, clearing ski trails, supervising work crews, training new sawyers, and working with timber sales. The work came naturally for him. His dad was a timber cutter. In the winter, he was a ski patrolman, and was patrol director for eighteen years. He was responsible for teaching expert skiing skills, first aid and safety, toboggan handling, lift evacuation—everything a ski patrolman has to know in order to handle any emergency on the slopes.

Hinkley also continued his love of gelande jumping.

Geleandessprung became popular in 1964 at Alta, Utah, but quickly spread throughout the skiing world. Some gelande jumpers gain speeds approaching 60 mph and flying distances in excess of 250 feet. In 1976, Paul Hitchcock recorded the longest jump on the 70-meter hill at Purgatory, 229 feet.

Dirty did more than jump competitively. In the 1978 movie, *Avalanche*, he was a stunt jumper. It was filmed at Purgatory and starred Rock Hudson and Mia Farrow. Cameras rolling, he landed 100 feet downslope, knees bent and skis skimming the surface of the snow. Suddenly he whipped into a violent cartwheel, sending his skis flying off before coming to a stop. In the silence that followed, Dirty slowly stood, then smiled, and walked off.

Taking hard falls and facing down danger was nothing new to him.

Dirty can reel off story after story of accidents that have happened when felling trees. Folks might think they can predict where and how a tree will fall as they cut it. But people like Dirty, with years of experience, know better. There was the time a falling tree hit the lift line, sending empty chairs flying, the time a falling tree chased him downhill, and worst of all, the time a member of the crew was killed by a tree as it fell.

"You're not out of the woods," Dirty explained, "until you're out of the woods."

The BD&M Expressway honors contributions of Dirty, Major Lefebvre, and Boudreaux Miller for their work building and maintaining trails and patrolling the mountain.

"DIRTY" DON HINKLEY

Robert W. (George) Smith

Tony Schweikle

59

Summer on the Mountain:
Plenty of ways to slide, glide, and fly

By the mid-1980s, more and more visitors had discovered the beauty of Purgatory and the fun available at the resort and in the surrounding San Juan Mountains for their summer vacations and recreation.

Maestro Mischa Semanitzky approached Purgatory with the idea of a classical music festival set in the mountains above Durango. Additional sponsors including Fort Lewis College, The Durango Herald, Morley Ballantine, and the Bank of Colorado were recruited, and in 1987 the inaugural "Music in the Mountains" classical music festival was launched. Its first season included five concerts and featured just eleven musicians, all from the Dallas Fine Arts Chamber Players.

The festival grew rapidly, attracting both local and regional audiences while also increasing the number of musicians, concerts, and venues. Now it features more than 220 world-renowned musicians, full symphony as well as smaller chamber concerts, non-classical feature performances, a conservatory for aspiring student musicians and a "Music in the Mountains Goes to School" program that reaches more than 4,000 elementary, middle, and high school students throughout the Four Corners region.

The festival and continuing growth in the resort's summer wedding and conference business helped spawn a steady increase in summer activities and amenities as well.

Mountain biking came to the resort in a big way when Purgatory hosted the first ever World Mountain Bike Championships in 1990. This led to an expansion of the resort's mountain-bike trails.

Next mini-golf course and disc golf courses were added to the core alpine slide attraction. Then a series of plaza activities, including bungee trampoline, climbing wall, and bounce house were added. The iconic Village Center Tower was converted into the launch platform for the Purgatory Plunge zipline. Riders zip above the "beach" area to a landing platform built from former lift towers and steel parts.

More plaza activities followed, including an aerial adventure course, water runners, mechanical bull, and gyro. Additional festivals have included a Mushroom Hunt and "foodie" festival, a Muck & Mire adventure mud race, and several other music, race, and family-oriented events. Most recently, the resort opened the Divinity Mountain Bike Flowtrail, the Four Corners' first lift-served downhill mountain-bike trail, to rave reviews.

Over time, summers at Purgatory have grown to the point that they attract more overnight guests than winter. The range of summer activities creates an amazing energy in the resort's base area and in the surrounding community from Memorial Day through the fall color season.

Scott DW Smith

Scott DW Smith

Scott DW Smith

Scott DW Smith

Scott DW Smith

In 2016, Music in the Mountains will celebrate its thirtieth season. Although the festival has grown to include multiple venues, Purgatory remains a favorite with artists and audience alike. The festival tent offers not only excellent acoustics, but also an intimate setting in which performers and patrons are quite close to one another.

Music in the Mountains photos

JUDY WACHOB

Judy Wachob had worked with Vern Greco for ten years while he was CEO at Steamboat Ski Resort. So a year after he moved to Purgatory as CEO, she joined him.

She's been at Purgatory ever since—twenty-one years now.

She started as director of ticket operations and then became director of skier services. That was followed by stints overseeing guest services along with the ticket operations before she became senior director of village services. In 2008, Judy was named vice president of village services—the first woman VP at the resort.

Greco wasn't replaced as CEO after he left for Park City in 1998. Rather, the resort was managed by an interim advisory committee, which included Judy as a member.

"Without a CEO" Judy said, "we ran our departments as a team."

The arrangement worked out quite well for two reasons: the directors and managers each understood their own areas of responsibility, and everyone was willing to "step up."

"It's always been that way," she said, recalling that she realized when she first arrived at Purgatory that she was joining a cooperative family. "We all help each other and we always have."

Judy appreciates that the pattern of mutual help and the sense of family it engenders are "as strong today as it ever was."

Women have not encountered a glass ceiling at Purgatory. In fact, Judy noted, many of the directors and managers are females—in charge of patrol, ski school, transportation, retail, and human resources, for instance. Nor is there any issue with gender discrimination.

"We don't look at each other as male or female," she said. "It's a very comfortable, safe environment."

Judy is excited, too, about Purgatory's new owner, James Coleman. He is a frequent visitor in the offices, shares employees' passion for the resort, and has "a vision and a plan" for its future.

Having worked at another ski area, Judy is especially mindful of how exceptional Purgatory and its employees are.

"It's just a different feel," she said. "We all want to do what's good for the guest and the ski area—working together and having fun."

"People have really come together for the common good [and] made it possible for us to do things I wouldn't even attempt now. . . . both in terms of recreation and also in terms of skiing."

– Dolph Kuss,
ski coach

Coming of age

A ski area and much more

By the late 1990s, Purgatory had weathered some tough challenges and the Duncan family realized it was time to bring in new investors. Chuck Cobb, a veteran resort and real estate developer/operator, who had been a minority owner at nearby Telluride, had expressed interest in the resort, and came on as a majority investor in 2000. Cobb already owned Kirkwood Mountain Resort (near Lake Tahoe, California). He saw the opportunity for synergies between the two mid-size resorts and the opportunity to grow the resort's bedbase to help make it more economically sustainable.

Cobb and his partners brought a new energy to Purgatory, initially by bringing in Kirkwood CEO Gary Derck to rejuvenate the operations and oversee the next wave of improvements. His task would be to guide future mountain improvements as well as develop a diverse, year-round, family-friendly recreational community on the lands acquired through the exchange.

At the heart of their vision for Purgatory was the now widely embraced principle of smart growth. The concept, which developed as a response to uncontrolled, sprawling development and its resultant problems, has gone by a variety of names, including new urbanism and managed growth. Universal among them are the commitment to creating walkable, mixed-use communities that will conserve resources, foster economic health, and promote safety. Other key characteristics are a strong sense of place, collaboration with stakeholders, open space, a range of housing choices, accessible transportation, and compact building designs. Even the US Environmental Protection Agency praises smart growth as "development that serves the economy, the community, and the environment."

The new owners started with the

base area and front side, where they identified several issues that needed immediate attention. Their plan was to improve the ski experience by creating a physical environment that would both accentuate and complement the spectacular mountain setting.

The first step was installation of a new detachable, high-speed six-pack lift (replacing the old Lift 1) which changed the way the front side of the mountain could be skied. Lovingly known as the "six-pack," the new lift was officially named the Purgatory Village Express and drew renewed attention to favorite front-side runs like Paradise, Styx, Hades, Pandemonium, and Catharsis, all mainstays of the original ski area.

Next came the tunnel under Shoel Street, making it possible for people to move from the main (upper) base village to the Columbine area without crossing a road at-grade. Following that came upgrades to the resort's arrival court, main pedestrian plaza and its famous "beach" area—the flat area at the base of the lifts where resort guests gather both winter and summer to people-watch and enjoy the views.

This was topped off by Purgatory Lodge, part of a $50 million-plus base village investment that

Charles E. "Chuck" Cobb brought a unique skill set and perspective when his Cobb Partners Group bought majority interest in Purgatory in 2000.

He had served as the CEO of numerous companies—including Walt Disney Development—as well as holding positions on a multitude of public and private boards, educational institutions, and in government. This Floridian was well prepared for winter, having been an owner in Telluride and served three years as US ambassador to Iceland. (Ambassador's Glade, on the mountain's front side, is named in honor of Chuck and his wife Sue, who served as ambassador to Jamaica.)

Chuck considers Durango a "spectacular town," with better restaurants than Telluride, the best weather, and "along with Snowmass, the best intermediate skiing in the Rockies." That doesn't mean Purgatory should aspire to be another Vail or Aspen.

CHARLES E. "CHUCK" COBB

> Purgatory's not trying to appeal to the elite, the top five percent, but it has to be high-quality. It has to be nice. Our prices in real estate will not be the same as Aspen or Vail, our prices of the lift tickets will not be as high, and the price of the dinners will not be as much. But Purgatory can still be four, four-and-a-half stars—and ideal for families.

Chuck noted that Purgatory's earnings have grown every year since 2000. But economic growth is not all that matters. His development and management of the resort is based on a philosophy that has become the watchword of developers all over the country. Following "smart growth" principles has enabled him to develop more than thirty new towns and master-planned communities. All share an emphasis on a strong sense of place, preservation of open space, variety of housing options, walkability, transportation, and compact designs.

In turn, the sense of community creates a good experience for families by offering a variety of things they can enjoy, both individually and collectively. Great experiences lead to great memories, which will bring people back again and again, not just for skiing but throughout the year.

Chuck embraced another invaluable principle as well: "Don't borrow more than you earn." Failure to follow that important lesson had brought Purgatory to the brink of financial ruin in the 1990s.

Even when the US suffered its worst economic downturn in decades, Purgatory carried on. "We hunkered down," Chuck says. "We kept our debt levels to twenty-five percent of our assets. A lot of resort developers will go fifty to sixty percent, and then when the cycle turns, a lot of them go broke."

Master Plan:
Patience and negotiation paid off

Creating a master plan for a 600+-acre community and 2,500 acres of federal permit area is challenging. But when you involve two separate counties, a metropolitan district, existing neighborhoods, rugged, steep terrain, and the challenges of building at almost 9,000 feet elevation, it can be daunting.

Under the guidance of CEO Gary Derck and a team of consultants and advisors, the community's master plan called for upgrading resort amenities and creating 1,649 new residential units as well as significant commercial space. Key aspects of the plan included clustering development in six distinct villages with forty percent of the land left as open space, providing a variety of housing types in relatively small bite-size phases, ensuring municipal quality infrastructure, and protecting wildlife habitat and environmental systems.

The plan was then incorporated into a development agreement that also addressed workforce housing for employees, air quality protections, a comprehensive recycling program, and an overall master association to manage the community in perpetuity. By 2002, the plan had been approved by both counties and the metro district.

In Colorado, development agreements can be challenged by members of the community provided they secure enough signatures on a petition. Colorado Wild, a local/statewide environmental group asserted the resort's commitments had not gone far enough in a few key areas. As a result, La Plata County voters had to vote on the development agreement. Negotiations between the resort and Colorado Wild yielded a settlement agreement that included incremental commitments on workforce housing, air quality, and the dedication of all of the resort's surface water rights in Hermosa Park to the Colorado Conservation Board. Colorado Wild then came out in support of the development agreement before the 2003 election, and the development agreement received broad voter approval.

However, that was only part of the process. While base area improvements could move ahead, changes on the mountain, which is mostly federal land, required a separate approval process. Under the direction of mountain manager Mike McCormack the management team set out to finalize an updated mountain master plan and environmental impact statement (EIS) for the Forest Service lands and mountain improvements. This process began with comprehensive environmental analyses focused on several issues including future improvements, mitigation of past damage from logging and grazing, erosion control, and vegetation management.

As the mountain improvement approval process moved along, the resort was able to work through several significant environmental issues/challenges, including mitigation protocol for the Canada Lynx, protecting the East Fork Hermosa Creek fishery, monitoring/mitigating erosion/sedimentation, and preserving scenic quality for adjoining public lands.

After seven long years of studies, public hearings, negotiations, and modifications, in January 2009, the Forest Service issued its record of decision approving the resort's new mountain master plan and EIS.

Shortly thereafter, in early 2010, the resort was awarded the National Ski Areas Association Silver Eagle award for excellence in fish and wildlife habitat protection by a ski resort. This is one of the ski industry's highest environmental honors.

includes luxury two-, three-, and four-bedroom residential units, a variety of new commercial shops and a slopeside restaurant dubbed "Purgy's." The building also included the Durango Mountain Club with a club lounge, family game room, fitness center, heated pool and water slide, spa, and lockers.

As Derck explained, "The club was the focal point of the community's social fabric, which in-cluded community and resort amenities to accelerate interaction and connection, creating a feeling of 'home' for residents."

It was important to the Cobb partners that Purgatory build on its year-round recreational offerings. Toward that end, they created "neighborhoods" focused on certain winter activities such as snowmobiling, nordic skiing, alpine ski-in/ski-out, and even snowshoeing. Summer and fall

activities grew to include not only the alpine slide and mountain biking, but also ziplines, an adventure course, bungee trampoline, horseback riding, fishing and hiking.

"There are just as many people who come up to Purgatory in the summer and maybe only come up in the winter two or three times. They have all that choice," Derck said.

The mountain also needed many upgrades and improvements, including an expanded snowcat grooming fleet, a multi-year snowmaking expansion, new gladed skiing on the back-side and front-side, and improvements to the learn-to-ski terrain. Rental facilities and equipment fleets were upgraded, restaurants renovated, and children's activities added—all focused on making Purgatory truly a great family destination.

As the master plan was progressing, the Cobb group used focus groups and outreach that emphasized the importance of reconnecting the resort with the town of Durango. The name Purgatory was retained for the mountain and ski operations while a new "Durango Mountain Re-

sort" brand was created to describe the broader community and the entire resort area from Tamarron/Glacier Club to Cascade Village, i.e. the "north county resort experience" in and around the base area and its surrounding lands.

A great deal of confusion resulted from these dual monikers. While the Durango Mountain Resort name helped the resort and resort community leverage the positive image of Durango as a popular mountain resort destination, locals felt the Purgatory name should still be at the forefront.

A marketing campaign was developed that focused on leveraging the unique family-friendliness of the resort and attracting new generations of families, under the vision statement of "Colorado Family Heaven." In just a few short years, from 2005 to about 2010, an incredible amount of improvements were constructed, transforming the base village and portions of the mountain into a new collection of amenities and experiences. Those changes drew the attention of regional and national press, and attracted new customers and locals to the family-friendly atmosphere.

The Cornell Family:
Rope tow romance

Family has been the keystone of Purgatory Resort from its inception. As the resort has grown over the years, so has its family.

Arizonans Paul and Renee Cornell first started dating at Purgatory in 1970-71, when they were students at Mesa Community College in Arizona. They founded a ski club and raised funds for a ski trip to Durango, then sat with one another on the bus and hung out together at Purgatory the entire time.

The couple remembers the beaver pond by the entrance road and the one double chair. Most of all, they remember how friendly everyone was. There was no beginners' area in those days, so fledgling skier Renee had to rely on a rope tow as Paul taught her the basics of the sport that would become a focus for them in the coming years.

The couple married and had two sons, and every year the family returned to Purgatory. They stayed at Needles, so they could be "right there" and get their fill of playing in the snow. To these desert dwellers, nothing could equal the peaceful, cozy feeling of fresh snow falling in the mountains.

Through the years, their attachment to Purgatory grew stronger. They started celebrating Thanksgiving here, then returning in January and over spring break. The boys and their parents developed an interest in mountain biking right around the time that Purgatory hosted the World Mountain Bike championships. They were thrilled to be able to ride the same course on the mountain in the summer.

The couple decided it was time to own a place on the mountain and found a condominium for a "reasonable price." As they spent more and more time at Purgatory, they formed lasting friendships with neighbors and Purgatory staff. It has become, in every sense of the word, a home for them. It has been especially gratifying to find the same people working in the ticket offices, lift lines and shops year after year.

"That tells us something about the resort," Paul said. "Employees love it up here and they stay here."

Their boys have grown now, graduated from college, married, and started their own families. The condo has become the ideal reunion spot, where everyone can enjoy hiking, biking, and skiing together. After all these years, the scenery still captivates them. Visits have become so frequent that Paul buys a season pass. After all, he does ninety percent of his skiing at Purgatory.

Like most people who are settled in their community, the Cornells do have some suggestions for improvements. A tunnel underneath the highway would make crossing the road to the mountain safe. And they would welcome more variety of restaurants close by.

As former Purgatory owner Chuck Cobb has said, "Purgatory is still a work in progress. It's only half-done."

MIKE McCORMACK

JIM "HOODY" HARDS

Many Purgatory employees have moved up the ranks through the years, people like **Jim "Hoody" Hards** and **Mike McCormack**.

Hoody came from Illinois in 1972 to attend Fort Lewis and ski at Purgatory. He was just seventeen and like many of his fellow student skiers, he never left. He began working part-time at Purgatory during his senior year, one of the "no-snow" years when the season opened the first week in January and closed in mid-February. He finished college in 1977 and started working full-time as a lift attendant. In the summer, he worked on lift operations and lift maintenance with fellow legends Keith Blackburn and Duane Bottoms.

From 1982 to 1987, Hoody advanced through a multitude of jobs: lift operations manager, guest services, ticket operations, and management of resort facilities. He also served on the Purgatory Metropolitan Board as a member and acting district manager. In 1987, Hoody was instrumental in establishing the Music in the Mountains festival at Purgatory, the most consistent event the resort has hosted. With the new ownership in 2000, he was involved in developing and getting the resort's master plan approved in 2002. Today, Hoody oversees base area operations, resort infrastructure, and construction for real estate projects.

In 1982, Hoody hired Durangoan Mike McCormack, originally in lift operations/maintenance. Mike quickly moved up the ranks: maintenance supervisor in 1987 and director of lift maintenance/operations in 1992. In 2000, he was promoted to vice president of mountain operations.

The two men have experienced many changes at Purgatory, from adding terrain and lifts to creating new summer attractions like the alpine slide, zipline, and mountain bike trails. The biggest changes have involved the advancement of technology within the ski industry and the evolution of the guest experience as ski resorts started competing with such other vacation options as cruise lines and theme parks.

In the 1990s, larger ski resorts began raising the bar, offering enhanced experiences both on and off the slopes. Purgatory adapted these initiatives by setting standards for employee appearance, improving the level of guest services and following a more comprehensive company mission statement.

"It's no longer just about skiing," Hoody said.

Throughout Mike's tenure, the mountain operations team has continually worked to utilize new technology, improving snowmaking infrastructure, grooming equipment, and chairlift mechanics. "Those improvements allow us to create a longer ski season with more consistent conditions, and deliver a better overall ski product to our guests," Mike said.

The most recent change on the mountain is the replacement of Legends Lift 8. Starting in December 2015, a new high-speed detachable quad chairlift will take skiers to Purgatory's summit in five minutes, where they will find new trails and additional snowmaking.

Hoody also keeps busy with real estate development at the resort. "Purgatory provides a beautiful setting and a very desirable place for a getaway," he said. "As much as it has changed, I think we'll always be a family-oriented, comfortable mountain destination."

PURGATORY
AT DURANGO MOUNTAIN RESORT

Colorado

Family

Heaven

Scott DW Smith photos

GARY DERCK

Gary Derck came to Purgatory as CEO in 2000 with a unique background. He started his career as a land planner/landscape architect, designing resort communities throughout the US. He then became a resort developer, building numerous golf-oriented communities in the West, after which he learned resort operations by running hotels, restaurants, and club amenities. Then, finally, he joined Chuck Cobb in 1999, to help run his mountain resorts.

Gary began as CEO of Kirkwood Mountain Resort in California in 1999 and took over at Purgatory as Chuck completed his negotiations with the Duncan family. He steered the resort through the creation of its new master plans, a community referendum, major base village and mountain improvements, and the 2008 recession. His negotiations with Colorado Wild demonstrate the importance he places on working with the broader community. Far from a "them vs. us" mentality, Gary viewed the protest as an opportunity to build consensus.

"Everybody's in this together," he said, "and we need the resort to work for everyone. We were able to tweak a few things that demonstrated our environmental commitment to do the right thing." Purgatory had to be forthcoming and earn voters' trust. Fortunately, people who had supported the ski area from the beginning spoke up, stressing how important it was to continue improving the resort. "In essence, locals reaffirmed the need for the resort to get better, just as the whole Durango region needs to get better," Gary said.

Gary has been determined, too, to maintain the family atmosphere that has always distinguished Purgatory, something he admits becomes increasingly challenging with growth. That includes providing housing programs and child care assistance for employees and rewarding the staff, as well as making guests feel welcome. "A happy staff makes for a happy resort, and a happy resort makes for happy guests," he explained.

Purgatory's vision statement "Colorado Family Heaven" describes what employees feel about the resort, according to Gary. In turn, their feelings allow Purgatory to "make it a reality for everyone" who comes to the resort.

Perhaps one of Gary's greatest challenges, and most significant achievements was the design and construction of Purgatory Lodge, which he personally led. Built over a former creek bed, the building had to provide all the support facilities that the resort was lacking—a great restaurant, a new ticket office, more shops, and a slope-side hang-out place as well as a beach-head location for property owners to have their own club facility. The result "transformed the resort's guest experience," according to Gary, by providing "a great place for everyone to begin or end their ski day, as well as a central gathering place for all the families who own property at the resort."

Those who visit on New Year's Eve will see that Durango now has its own "mini-Times Square," right at the base of Purgatory.

Scott DW Smith

Scott DW Smith

Scott DW Smith

Scott DW Smith

Scott DW Smith

Scott DW Smith

Scott DW Smith

"An average skier can move two tons of snow downhill in a day."
— Don "Boudreaux" Miller, director of trails

Foundation for the Future

Building on the legacy

As Chuck Cobb approached his eightieth year, he and his partners reached the decision to find a new steward of Purgatory Resort to continue its development. On October 29, 2014, the resort's management introduced James H. Coleman Jr. as the new principal owner of Purgatory, and on February 25, 2015, Coleman announced the return of the Purgatory name to Durango's ski mountain. One of his top priorities is to "expedite improvements in the approved mountain master plan," thereby ensuring the movement forward that marked recent years.

Purgatory Resort has grown significantly in the last fifty years. What started as a small local mountain with a single chairlift, a few trails, and a modified A-frame base lodge has grown to a 3,000+-acre multi-season resort and surrounding community that hosts 250,000+ winter visitors and 100,000+ summer visitors. It continues to have a very loyal local following, but now attracts visitors from throughout the US and abroad. Yet most of its customers still come from the southwestern US, and most still drive with their family . . . and their extended family and friends . . . to their favorite spot in the Colorado mountains.

The first fifty years have presented many challenges. Purgatory has weathered financial difficulties such as capital calls, bank negotiations, low snow years, oil industry declines, travel/tourism impacts and significant recessions. It has confronted environmental challenges such as rugged terrain, regulatory processes, political challenges, environmental policy shifts, and now climate change. And it has overcome human challenges such as deaths; retirements; and finding, retaining, and training staff—the right kind of employees—to maintain the resort's unique atmosphere.

Through it all, the unique sense of "family" and the resort's family-friendly culture and atmosphere have persevered. Family was imbedded in the first visions shared by Ray Duncan, his initial partners, and associates. It was strengthened through the initial hardships of building lifts, trails, and amenities with limited means, and where none had existed before. It has been passed on through different leaders and management teams as the resort grew, stumbled, got back on track, and continued to grow. And it is embodied in the spirits and camaraderie of thousands of local folks who worked at the resort, ran its operations, built its facilities, and battled the elements.

This sense of family has made those who visit feel incredibly comfortable and a part of the place . . . in some cases almost instantly. Parents have brought their kids to learn how to ski. And as the kids have grown up, they have brought their own kids back to their favorite mountain . . . to learn where they learned . . . and to experience what they had experienced.

Now, generations of families gather to celebrate their special family traditions in the San Juan Mountains above Durango, enjoying the town and the resort that has become a part of their legacy and such an important part of their lives.

There is much more to come for Purgatory. The foundation has been set on a solid base of beauty, adventure, quality, caring, and sharing. And with the completion of the new Legends Lift 8, the skiing experience will be better than ever.

See you on the mountain!

Preceding page: The SixPack whisks skiers to the top on a snowy morning.
Scott DW Smith

Facing page: Skiers on the way down to the base area have a panoramic view of the Twilight Peaks.

LACKBURN'S BASH ◇→

←RAY'S RIDGE ◇

"We're not going to rest on
what we are now."

**- Gary Derck
CEO Purgatory Resort**

Afterword

Dear Reader,

Purgatory is a special place built by people with vision and a heart for the mountains. It is one of the most unique ski resorts on the planet with its stair-stepped slopes and world-class views. The Duncan family and many others, some of whose names grace our trails, worked with incredible voracity in the early years and made Purgatory a name recognized around the country.

James Coleman

This is the place I advanced as a skier faster than ever, on my second ski trip, during my sophomore year in high school. I remember those first turns looking out towards Engineer like it was yesterday, then finding Styx . . . I had found heaven on earth! Purg's character certainly had something to do with my increased rate of progression. It definitely fueled my passion for skiing and by the time I was a senior in high school I had made the decision to pursue a dream of developing ski areas in the Southwest. What an honor to be entrusted with this responsibility right here.

The future for Purgatory is very bright. Chuck and Sue Cobb put together a team that successfully weathered the greatest recession of our time and obtained significant approvals that positioned the resort for substantial improvements for years to come. The first of many steps begins this year with the upgrade of the Legends lift to a high-speed quad. Purg will see annual improvements to lifts, trails, snowmaking, summer activities, lodging, and other facilities. These improvements will take the resort to a new level of convenience and fun to share with our family and friends.

So many people helped build Purgatory into what it is today, and we are truly grateful for their contributions. Our 50th Anniversary Celebration, combined with our return to the Purgatory name, is a fitting tribute to their hard work, dedication and perseverance. Thank you for the amazing memories!

**Sincerely,
James Coleman**

Preceding page: The base area is a far cry from opening day fifty years ago, when it had one double chair, a Poma lift and the Day Lodge.
Scott DW Smith

Facing page: Pandemonium provides a view straight down to the base area with Spud Mountain in the background.

References

Printed Sources

Blair, Robert, *The Western San Juan Mountains: Their Geology, Ecology, and Human History*, Niwot, CO: University Press of Colorado, 1996.

Butler, Ann, "'Inferno' and Who's Who - Purgatory's names reflect its past," *Durango Herald*, March 22, 2014.

Langdon, Charlie, *Durango Ski: People and Seasons at Purgatory*, Durango, CO: Purgatory Press, 1989; reprint: Durango, CO: Durango Herald Small Press, 2007.

McDaniel, Robert, "A High Country Ranch in the Depression," *Historic Durango*, 2009.

Philpott, William, *Vacationland: Tourism and Environment in the Colorado High Country*, Seattle, WA: University of Washington Press, 2013.

Pinchot, Gifford, *The Use of the National Forests*, US Department of Agriculture, 1907.

Platt, Kalvin V*., Master-Planned Communities: Lessons from the Developments of Chuck Cobb*, Urban Land Institute, 2011.

Smith, Duane A. *Rocky Mountain Boomtown: A History of Durango, Colorado*, Boulder: University Press of Colorado, 1992.

Uroda, Deborah, "Town Ski Area Can Grow Apart–or Together, *Durango Herald*, July 21, 1985.

Uroda, Deborah, "Two Shops are Better than One...," *Durango Herald*, July 22, 1985.

Interviewees

Chester "Chet" Anderson
Karen Bell
Bob Blackburn
Mary Jane, Jackson Jr., and Antonia Clark
Charles E. "Chuck" Jr. and Sue Cobb
Paul and Renee Cornell
Gary Derck
Joella Dunagan
Randy Dunagan
Raymond T. Duncan
Paul Folwell
Jim "Hoody" Hards
Bob Hill
"Dirty" Don Hinkley
Carlyn Hodges
Eric Hodges
Mickey Hogan
Adolph "Dolph" Kuss
Ruel "Major" Lefebvre
Mike McCormack
Don "Boudreaux" Miller
Kim Morton
Mary Lou Murray
John Ogier
Richard L. Peterson
Judy Wachob

Archival Sources

Bayfield Ranger District records, San Juan National Forest

Delaney Southwest Research Library and Archives, Center of Southwest Studies, Fort Lewis College
    Purgatory Collection, P066
    Nina Heald Webber Southwest Colorado collection, M194 and P056
    San Juan National Forest virtual archive, M080
    Southwest Colorado photograph collection, P001
    Charlie Langdon Oral History Collection, U024

Index